Social Media Marketing Mastery: Increase Your Website Traffic, Grow Your Business, and Earn More Money

Table of contents

Power of social media

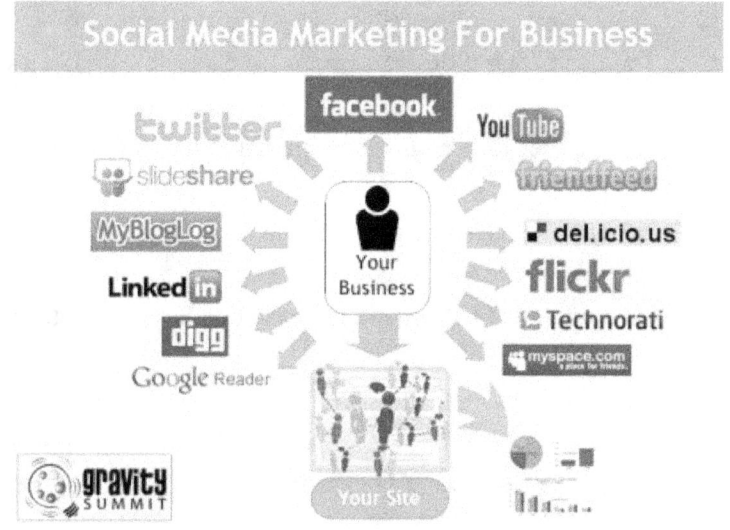

There is no proper definition of social media and it is due to the fact that the internet is regarded as the sole platform of social media and this is a place that has always been the favorite channel for businesses and corporations to interact with their employees and customers. The point which most of the businesses ignore is that social media is a place where you have to work, work and work. If someone claims that you can grow the business or triple the sales overnight then it is a big lie which is never to be believed. There is not a single strategy in this virtual world of business which can make it possible for the business to increase revenue or sales within a short period of time.

The fact is that if this platform is used sensibly and in a strategic manner then only a business can make sure that positive results are gained. The power of social media can only be utilized if the business is selling something worth purchasing. In other words it is the quality which matters so if the business is not offering something which is of high standard then you can never build an audience on social media. Even if you manage to create a solid platform it will be destroyed with the passage of time as people will start leaving. There is no need to work hard when it comes to social media rather a business needs to work smart.

If you are a using this platform to attain new and potential customers then beware of the fact that it is a very brutal platform that consumes a lot of time. Most of the business or even individual users fail at this point and hence fail to capture a very large market.

Despite of all these facts social media is a very powerful tool to promote a product as well as business. Below are some highlights that would provide a better picture in this regard:

- Facebook, the largest social media network of the world is just 10 years old and has a count of 800+ million daily active users according to a report published in September 2014.

- Twitter is just 8 years old and according to the stats it published in December 2014 daily active user base of this social media network is 284 million.

- Google+ definitely needs no introduction. Backed by the power of Google this social media platform has almost 600 million active users as per stats of October 2014.

So now you can well imagine the fact that how social media can

transform the business as well as sales by bringing together

diversity from all around the world at NO COST.

SMM or social media market proven strategies for all platforms

Social media market or SMM is based on several strategies that vary from platform to platform but there some common points that every social media marketer has to follow i.e. quality and engagement. These factors are interrelated due to the fact that a business can engage users only if quality posts are written. Getting more fans is not a big deal if the SMM specialist is posting relevant and state of the art content on social media. Before we delve deep into the subject it is important that we merge the SMM strategies as well as different social media websites intro so that it

becomes easy for the readers to apply then in a stellar fashion

getting the best out of this e-book.

Facebook

Introduction

Facebook was launched worldwide in 2005 however the development phase was completed in 2004. Today this website is the largest in the world in terms of users and daily traffic so for all businesses irrespective of their size it is a boon. According to a report published by Facebook in July 2014 it has 1.3 billion active users from all over the world making it the largest social media platform as well.

Paid advertisement

Most of the people are of the view that paid marketing on

Facebook is very costly and hence they back off. The fact of the

matter is that paid advertisement on Facebook is close to free.

Most of the large website hosting companies and other

organizations provide Facebook advertisement coupons and these

coupons are available through other websites as well like Fiverr

and Freelancer. Normally a $50 coupon costs $5 which in return

attracts or notifies a huge chunk of potential customers. Facebook

coupons are of two kinds one having an expiry date of several days

and the second ones having expiry date of few hours so before you

purchase a coupon make sure that seller provides you a guarantee

that it will work. This aspect of Facebook paid marketing is

something that most SMM specialists do not know so apply it to

make sure that you get the best in terms of user engagement and

page likes.

Paid advertisement is a part of Facebook that requires a business to spend a small amount to get large audience. But it could be done for free if an SMM specialist knows how to manipulate the friend request phenomenon, use following points to get much better results over a period of time:

- **A great cover photo** great in the sense that it should be in line with the business or page requirements. NEVER upload a picture that is taken from Google images or any other copyright free source as it will never create an impact user wants to feel. Develop and design images yourself or hire a designer to get the job done

- **Continuous posting** is one of the key factors that would make sure that the page engagement is also tested at different parts of day. It is also one of the biggest mistakes which individuals and businesses make i.e. posting of content in local business hours. One thing that an SMM specialist needs to consider is the fact that the business relations developed through social media are cross border so pot relevant content throughout day and night to make sure that customers feel that the business cares.

- **Crowdfunding** is one of the best Facebook marketing strategies that let the customers speak. It is not just collection of funds but if you are launching a new product or service then let the customers decide the name and nature of the brand. This will create a strong engagement and customers will be more than happy to assist the business they are engaged with.

- **Profile picture** says a lot about the page without speaking much. The current alignment of FB page creation is such that the profile picture is embedded within the cover photo so always choose a picture that matches the cover photo. All the rules of cover photo are applied to the profile picture as well i.e. be creative and never use image that saves money i.e. a copyright free image from Google images or any other source.

- **Call to action** is the best thing that engages the users and it can be done with the help of posts that you often write to the page. Business should always try to make sure that each and every post is embedded with a clear and concise call to action. For example see one of the posts below:

"Click like and comment to vote for the upcoming

concert destination".

This post has a clear call to action for all the users who see it.

More interest can be added by posting an additional line i.e.

"And get free tickets through lucky draw. For

more details visit [the website or page URL]"

Now a clear call for action will automatically drive customers to

visit the page and resultantly you will enjoy a dual effect,

Facebook page win and more traffic towards the website.

- **Replying fans** as it is one of the greatest strategies that

  encourage the customers to ask more questions. It can

  also be regarded as one of the basic and first steps

  towards the brand management on social media. When

  a user comes up questions he or she also makes sure to

  complain if not satisfied with a particular feature. It

  will thus allow you to upgrade the product features so

that you get more engagement ultimately leading to website traffic.

- **Automation kills** and this is a fact which you cannot overlook. Though Facebook allows the business to automate the posts but it is recommended to most of the businesses not to use it. There is a possibility that you might have posted something when it is night in the town but day in another country. Posting breeds questions and for the same reason it is very important to for the page owner to answer them. If they don't the user engage is hampered to a great extent.

Quick View

13% of organizations are looking to hire experienced staff to manage their social media activities.

14% are measuring the effectiveness of using social media in relation to their business

15% are responding highly positively to the social media outcomes that they got as a result of implementation.

22% of the organizations are conducting training sessions for the staff to educate them.

25% are spreading awareness in the organization regarding the use of social media.

31% are of the view that social media is a revenue generator for the company.

41% of the total businesses are of the view that social media has a sober impact on position of the company.

Facebook marketing strategies on large corporate level

Unfortunately most of the small businesses apply the strategies of large corporate level, waste time and then they quit. The fact of the matter is that small businesses don't have as much room as large corporations have and the credit goes to their overall structure as well as maintenance of mass level social media activities. On large corporate level stats are analyzed in depth to devise sound strategies for coming years where this action is never required by small organizations. Following are some strategies that are very important when it comes to large organizations:

- Giving the fans a reason to stay on the page should be the first and foremost strategy of large corporation. This can be easily done by offering free coupons, online purchasing as well as high level information that others don't have about any particular product or service.

- Large corporations can engage more users and can boost sales by making sure that they share and celebrate their milestones with the customers. Take a look at the post below:

  "Like & share this post and get a chance to meet with the CEO of our company as a part of our 50th anniversary celebrations (through lucky draw)."

This post compels the users to like and share post to make sure that enter the lucky draw. Apart from this strategy large corporations can also share posts with minimum timelines to see how users respond. Take a look:

  "Like this post within next 10 minutes and get a chance to win XYZ product through a lucky draw"

Users will now make sure that the post is liked as soon as possible so that they can enter the lucky draw, this strategy is still being deployed by large organizations like Dell, Wal-Mart and Vodafone and the results are definitely awesome.

- **Sharing stories** is one of the best ways to engage users. On corporate level business stories come into being everyday so they should make sure that a story which helps others with some product or their own personal business. Tips to run successful business or user capturing can also be engaging for large chunk of audience in this regard.

Organizations should consider their Facebook page as their sole business network and for the same reason they should also make sure that trend is measured to make sure that users are fully indulged.

Taking SMM to next level

In 2015 social media pros are of the view that not only Facebook but other social media websites will have a significant impact on the business to make sure so next level marketing is very important. The importance of the phenomenon can be judged by the fact that in 2015 almost 50-55% users will search social media as well as the internet before making a purchase which shows ever increasing importance of this channel. Following are some tips that most of the businesses never follow considering them as trivial but the fact of the matter is that in coming years these tips and tricks will allow both small and large users to get increasing number of fans as well as loyal customers:

- **Pinned posts:** There are some posts which users like a lot and the success can also be measured with the help of different application like Wildfire. A business should pin that particular post that has generated relatively high traffic ratio as compared to others and this process should be repeated every week.

- **Success review:** For any business it is very important to make sure that success on social media is measured with the help of qualified staff. Not only the short comings and issues will be judged but it will also allow the business to devise those strategies that are vital for online business expansion.

- **Give incentive:** A social media fan will only subscribe to a business's email listings or newsletters if he gets an incentive. The business should make sure that something additional is provided to the people who are getting off the social and onto the email listings.

Points to ponder

29% of the total ineffective users say that social media has no value in business.

50% of the total users who somehow manage to achieve the target say that the corporation does not take social media very seriously.

57% are saying that organization is getting the sense to use social media.

61% demand that the staff should be trained as there is a learning gap.

And 69% of B category says that the growth rate of social media marketing will increase in coming years.

32% of the total effective users say that social media has a vital importance which is given by the top management of the company.

42% are of the view that using social media in making marketing strategy is of vital importance to the organization.

Common errors in Facebook marketing

As mentioned before there is no way by using which you can gain page fans overnight. It is due to the fact that the best strategy involves working on continuous basis so that results are fruitful. One of the most common errors in conducting SMM through Facebook is getting fake or false likes. Even if they are given by real users they bring zero value to the business as freelancing sites like Fiverr and PeoplePerHour.com sell Facebook likes for very cheap rates so the users indulged with the page will never boost as they have been manipulated by the freelancer and there is also a possibility that the fans gained in this way will leave without notice. The usual rate is $5 to $10 per 3000 to 4000 likes but they are never recommended as they will hamper the online success and business will not be able to draw a clear line between legit and illegitimate users.

Social media is not as easy as most of the businesses think so chances of success are zero if SMM specialist steps into the market without clear goal as well as strategy. Unluckily most newbie SMM professionals succumb after wasting several days and getting nothing out of SMM. In order to become an SMM pro it is very important to run all campaigns under different plans so that effectiveness can be attained in a well-defined manner. It is to be noted that *13% of organizations are looking to hire staff to manage their social media activities* which shows that how seriously these companies are looking towards this platform. The need of the hour for all SMM managers, pros and professionals is to make sure that they upgrade their knowledge frequently. This is due to the fact that ***half of the knowledge of SMM is outdated after every 90 days.*** This also shows the rapidness of the new and emerging methods in this field so it is very important for SMM specialists to get the best knowledge as well as certifications such as Google Adwords and other private SMM certifications that are offered online.

Another fatal mistake when it comes to SMM is lack of dialogue marketing. Dialogue marketing foster two way communications and for the same reason both business and the customer communicate with each other to make the relation strong. If this factor is ignored then gaining more fans is never possible for the business when it comes to social media. Absence of dialogue marketing makes a customer think that the business is not ready to listen to him or he is not the part of the page. ***Business should remember that unliking a page is as simple as liking it.***

Despite of huge power and success stories of social media most of the businesses do not take this medium of interaction seriously and for the same reason they fail to reach a competitive market full of potential customers. Social media and all the related metrics should be added to the marketing strategy of the business so that social media managers as well as the marketing departments take it seriously and develop solutions that bring inevitable success to business streams resulting in increased revenue. Targeted posts and users will also act as indirect marketers for the business and if the

strategy is devised in the best possible manner then the results are

beyond predictions. The Facebook page should look like a store

front which compels a user to buy a particular or service from the

business so it should be attractive and convincing.

Twitter

Introduction

With 8th rank worldwide according to a report published by Twitter it has approximately 300 million daily active users from all over the world hence a huge markets waits for all those businesses that are unaware of the power of social media. Twitter was launched in 2006 and therefore the website is just 8 years old. The registration of the website is free of cost and it has been estimated that about 80% of world's famous brands have created their accounts on the website to interact with the customers.

Marketing with Twitter

Twitter is one of the simplest social platforms that make it possible for the businesses to access large customer chunks and therefore it has been into the limelight since long. *According to expert social media strategists Twitter should be used for customer services instead of marketing as state of the art and prompt resolutions regarding any product or service itself is the greatest marketing*

29

strategy when it comes to the internet and social media. However it is very important to follow certain simple rules and steps to make sure that a business gets most out of this awesome platform. Following are some of these steps.

- **Keeping it simple** is the most important point as Twitter is a micro blogging site. It allows sending messages that are 160 characters long. But it never means that full 160 character strength should be used to deliver the message. For good marketing of business via Twitter it is important for the business to keep the tweets below 100 to 110 characters. Surveys in this regard show that simple and concise tweets gain 17% more attraction as compared to long ones.

- **Use of hash tags** should be done with care. Formerly the SMM strategies of the businesses included use of extensive hash tags but now the scenario has changed a lot. A business should use not more than 2 hash tags.

It is now a wrong thinking that more hash tags foster large customer base that follow the business.

- **Reaching people organically** is the best way for a business to grow the audience. Stellar businesses always focus on loyal customer base and therefore they never allow any illegitimate strategy to hammer their online presence for instance purchasing Twitter following.

- **Customer services** is a key to success and for the same reason it is very important for the business to maintain an online platform solely for customer services and taking Twitter features into account it is the best option in this regard. As soon as any person has posted a comment, favored a tweet, done any retweet the account operator gets an instant message and for the same reason prompt resolution of the issue and reply is possible. All the print market done by the company should include twitter account name printed on it so that people get to know that the business is using its Twitter account solely for the purpose of customer care.

- **Images embedded in Tweets** is the most effective way making sure that the retweet rate increases. The report that has been published by Twitter itself reveals unbelievable facts. *Tweets having photos embedded receive 150% more engagement and retweets as compared to text only tweets.*

- **Choosing multiple time zones for tweets** is also one of the next level strategies for engaging audience on Twitter. Similarly posting old stuff again also reaches new customers and makes it possible for the business to get more followers. *Stats in this regard show that posting same content multiple times engages new* *users 75% more as compared to new content*

creation.

- **A/B test** should be performed to make sure that the best results are generated that would serve the business for longer period of time. This test can be conducted by posting two separate tweets with slight time difference usually couple of hours. Results in this regard show that *tweets done in morning or in the afternoon engage more users as compared to other times.*

- **Never use auto tweet sender** due to the fact that large business has millions of followers who are living in different time zones and a new tweet instantly gets massive response. If any user asks a solid question and the business is not there to answer then it is not a good sign for a successful social media campaign.

- **Extract audience** and engage more followers. This can be done by running Twitter Ad campaigns. This is never done on consumer level instead this point is used to make sure that other businesses that have shown interest in product or service are engaged. To achieve the goal a Twitter Ad partner account and a Twitter Ads account should be purchased.

- **Reframing Tweets** is a time saving strategy that makes sure that personalized tweets are sent to the users without much effort. For using this method in an effective manner it has been advised to all the businesses to reduce the tweet characters to 110 maximum as it allows the followers to retweet them by adding personal comments and sometimes the business finds a gem out of the personalization done.

Important statistics

_21% of the users say that tools provided by a certain platform do
not meet the business requirements_

_69% businesses have outsourced SMM to the marketing
companies._

_43% businesses trust the abilities of communication companies
when it comes to maintaining social media accounts._

_35% companies and small businesses believe that social media is a
part of public relations_

_30% users are of the view that SMM is the work of qualified web
professionals._

_17% businesses have sales departments or companies that are
managing the task for them._

_12% of the companies have hired customer services to carry out
SMM for them._

It is also to be noted that effective use of Twitter account not only boosts sale but over the period of time it also makes it possible for the business to get loyal additions to their email listing as well. There are certain strategies that used to work in the past but now they are never recommended as they sent a message to the followers that they have been hoodwinked into the process.

Twitter Strategies that are to be avoided

- **Inorganic practices**

First and foremost practice that was used to gain quick following in the past was to play with the psychology of the people. A person used to follow a certain person or company and in return the second party also used to follow the first one. The second party was then unfollowed by the first one after a few days. This was usually done with the help of automated bots and manually. Today the user is very different from what they used to be a couple of years before. Now people also keep an eye on their following so this tip is never recommended when it comes to corporate level as it is considered as a blunder. People will definitely follow the business but once they are unfollowed they will not only leave the page but will also make sure that a negative impression of the business is spread. *A business should keep in mind that activities on all social media websites instantly go viral.*

- **Purchasing Twitter followers**

This practice was very common in SMM two years back but now it is not recommended. Social media presence is always judged by the traffic which it generates for the actual website so purchasing false following will never move the curve in a way business wants it to. Positivity can never be achieved in a false way so it is very important to make sure that this step is never repeated. In simple words a business or an individual who thinks that twitter influence

is measured by number of followers is absolutely WRONG as this

strategy has also ended the social media career of many small

organizations.

- **Replying every Tweet having business or certain service name**

When Twitter was launched in 2006 businesses and individuals

were not aware of the usage ad large corporate organizations also

used to reply each and every tweet mentioning their business name

or name of any service. Over the period of time as Twitter

launched new services and twitter usage guides were made this

practice became embarrassing so it is not practicable now and

therefore it is not recommended. It creates a negative impression of

a business and when it comes to large following keeping an eye

ball on each follower is not possible. Instead the business should

make sure that appropriate contact is made with the customer who

has tweeted anything that endangers the online reputation of the business as well as product. In other words business should response when and where necessary and not every time.

- **Never follow trends, be professional**

Following trends is a good thing and makes it possible for an individual user to get noticed but for any business it is never recommended. *According to Twitter 17% of total trends on the website end within an hour or sooner* so instead of wasting efforts in trivial activity it is recommended to get in touch with the users by discovering creative ways that engage users on continuous basis.

- **Pushing Tweets to other websites**

This strategy is also used to work in the past but now it's obsolete so it is never recommended to use it. The fact of the matter is that every website has its own different demographics and one strategy for all never works out. For instance the LinkedIn audience is most professional of all so posting a fun filled tweet on LinkedIn will not leave a good impact. Posts for every social media website are to be tailored according to the environment of the website. The second example is that Twitter and Facebook are noisy where as Pintrest and LinkedIn are calm so one strategy form both is neither applicable nor will it work. Tailor content according to the audience definitely requires time but if you are planning to capture Twitter for a very long period of time then follow the mentality of the audience. Take out sometime every day and make sure that individual posts for each social media network are created to match the need of the audience in a better way.

Taking Twitter SMM to next level

According to expert SMM specialists Twitter is not same as it was in 2006. The main reason and cause of this change is continuous awareness and it also makes it possible for the business to get next level assistance from the website by using its features in a very refined way to increase sales and engage users. The first and foremost tip in this regard is to make sure that the best content is distributed among the followers. Creating a brand personality is the second thing that is required in this regard and it is up to the SMM specialist of the company to create a virtual posture of the brand and then to make sure that all tweets are posted in such a manner that it matches the brand personality. In an ideal scenario what a business wants is a high click rate as well as website traffic website and it all can be achieved even if the tweets are not well decorated with images. All a business or the related SMM specialist needs is an approach that is strategic in nature and predicts the end result as well. If these results are even 60% achieved the strategy is considered to be successful.

In order to make sure that the best response is generated towards the main business website it is recommended to create a complete list of all keywords that explain the business or the related products. Once done SMM specialist should create tweets based in these keywords and in this regard *twitter reports show that relevant keywords compel people to click on the embedded links*

27% more as compared to other tweets. So a business should

consider keywords as a backbone of the content and social media

strategy, they should be used in an intelligent manner. If keywords

are embedded in a sensible manner then it is very important to note

that the number of characters is to be raised to 140.

Over the period of time statistics have shown that a business is

considered to be more effective if followers are retained rather

than making new ones. A business should make sure that effective

links are posted within tweets as they make it possible for the users

to gain access to something that is of value to them. From a

business point of view SMM specialist should post links regarding

trouble shooting of issues of different products or those which lead

the users to some resolution regarding a particular product.

Undoubtedly conversations are very important but in order to

retain followers a business should make sure that links are posted

more as compared to replies to generate conversations. The best

example in this regard is as follows:

"Take a look at our new range of designs [URL]"

This tweet clearly shows that a business is inviting the users to take actions which will automatically drive traffic towards the website. There is an element of mystery as well because Twitter is a platform where a business cannot generate multiple tweets to show each and every thing to its users. The fact is that conversations never generate followers as compared to link posting as people with the passage of time come to know that they are getting something they were looking for or adds some value. It can be an article or a YouTube video that leads them to answers they are looking for.

Most of the businesses of the field make sure to stick to their own brand which is a false and action less idea. Though the Twitter trends expire within few hours still the business should look for those issues which it can solve, no matter the product belongs to the rival. It will not only bring the Twitter account into the limelight but will definitely generate loyal followers due to the fact that their issue has been resolved. However this should be done in a very careful manner to avoid backfire.

Twitter marketing strategy also includes following the right people. It was definitely hard n the past but now it isn't. There are several tools available on the internet that leads a business towards a more targeted market. Tools like Follower wonk and Twellow allows a person or a business to find the right person and then follow them. The keywords optimization of these tools also make sure that right people interested in the brand are extracted so that the business can view their activities on Twitter. Once the process has been completed now it is the time to make sure that new people are indulged with the business. Tweeting with them and tweeting at them are two different ideas. Tweeting with them should be the strategy of the business in this regard to make sure that they follow the account back. These tools will also generate fresh lists everyday so it will lead the business to those who have talked about the brand for even once. Thanking each and every one of them, marking conversations as favorite are actions that will make sure that a loyal customer base is created who will continue following the business account for a very long period of time. According to the human psychology the people will also think that it was the business that came searching them and hence the element of loyalty automatically increases. Following this tip will also make sure that a business leads the social media as a brand ambassador of the industry retaining users and generating sales for as long as internet exists.

Twitter is based on the concept of icebreaking; it is an effortless action which makes sure that most of the people are indulged with the business. If the business account is bloating with 100,000 followers then it is very important to meet those one who are nameless. It can be done in a classic manner. All business relevant tweets should be retweeted, should be added to favorites and if the follower has posted a link then a similar link should be posted to him alone by adding @ [only name of the user]. It will instigate a chain reaction and those users who are of similar genre will make sure to tweet and retweet more to make sure that they become highlighted. Making the business page nosier should be first and foremost duty of the SMM specialist and if it is done for a period of 24/7/365 then not only the business has captured a large LOYAL following but the SMM specialist has also shown his prowess in a great manner.

Relationship building is one of the most important factors that help a business to spread their word over the internet. Once a healthy fan base has been generated then a business should never take it for granted. On every business page there are certain people that retweet the business more than others and in this way they become indirect marketers of the business. All such followers should be added to private listings. A business should also thank them by following them back as long as their tweets are relevant. Social media users are really smart nowadays and for the same reason great content is always shred on the business page so the business should make sure that this content is shared repeatedly. It will make sure that those conversations are generated that are business related. On the other hand it will also make sure that strong relationships are fostered with all such users. Business should make sure that all these users are personally contacted using Twitter so that more information is gathered about them in order to make sure that relationships based on trust and confidence are developed. This will also make sure that this customer base never leaves the page.

Google +

Introduction

After Facebook Google+ is the largest social network of the world. According to a report published in October 2014 Google+ has a daily active user base of 540 million so for all the businesses there are limitless opportunities on this social media platform. Backed by the power of Google this social media platform was launched in 2011 so it is just three years of age.

Basics of Google+ SMM strategy

First and foremost thing to be noted is that there are many

advantages of using Google+ as compared to other social media

websites. The most favorable advantage is that the activities

conducted on Google+ are automatically registered on Google

search engine so finding a business that is active on Google+ is not

a big deal if Google search engine is used. Secondly there are other

products which a business can take full advantage of like Google

maps. If the business has a physical location then it is very

important for the SMM specialist to make sure that this location is

added to Google+ page so that it is placed in the search engine

results once verified. Today SEO has become a complete industry

and for the same reason separate discussion is required in this

regard. For any SMM specialist it is good to have the SEO

knowledge but it is never necessary so assuming that the person

does not have SEO knowledge still it is easy to get to the power of

Google+ by following one simple tip i.e. adding relevant keywords

in all the posts of Google+ and at the same time making sure that website links and related blog articles, their keywords and website content should be added. Like Twitter Google+ also makes it possible for the users to add hash tags. These hash tags should be the keywords so that the page is ranked high on Google search engine and ultimately once a user comes through Google search engine he will not only follow the page but will also visit the website to get more knowledge. So in this way Google's power of SEO will drive more traffic and increasing conversion rate as well. SEO might be tough for some but when it comes to Google+ it is not.

As Google is the sole owner of this multipurpose platform a business should make sure that site is connected with the Google+ page and it is one of those strategies which many businesses never follow and resultantly the conversion rate is low despite this awesome platform. Keywords in this regard also play an important role and for the same reason it is very important to note that the page or business description should be keyword enriched but SMM should not be overwhelming with keywords as the results can backfire and the rank of the page might drop if Google changes the strategy which it does quiet often. Keywords will automatically interact with the Google Ad words and the most searched items on the search engine so more optimization means more users to your page and hence more revenue generation. SMM strategy should also include the page verification and if the business is large with thousands of followers then the Google+ contacts the page owner to make sure that the page is legit. A verified page brings more customers and allows the business to groom in the best possible manner. *Analysis show that a Google+ page optimized to deliver the message receives 40% higher visits as compared to other social media websites.*

Posting via Google+ is easier as compared to other social media websites as it allows the business to maintain the content in a way a business wants it to look. Lengthy blog posts attract more users as compared to shorter ones and increase the conversion rate as well.

For all image embedded post lovers Google+ is a boon as it does not crop or changes the size of the images. On the other hand it also makes sure that the post goes through the eyes of more customers as compared to the ones that are text only. No matter whatever the room or size of the image is Google+ will not only adjust it but will also make sure that the size remains the same and there are no changes made in this regard. It is simply one of the best and awesome features of Google+ in this regard.

Adding those pagers that are relevant to the business is also one of the best strategies of all times. It will allow the business to keep an eye on the activities of these pages so the best strategies are chosen for the platform. Another thing which most of SMM specialists are unaware of is that larger size of community on Google+ will make sure that the impact is also great so that the people following can be indulged in different way and it is only Google+ which ensures such business pages are ranked high on Google search engine which have large communities so that their exposure as well as the overall impact on the internet increases. So when it comes to Google+ the first and foremost target of any business should be to gain more followers and once it has been done then the second target is to retain the existing followers and to make sure that new ones are also invited in different ways. Logically speaking if the content of the business is great but the fan following is low then it is of no use so in order to create awesome effect on Google+ the SMM strategy should include gathering more and more people to enjoy the dual impact of high page ranks on Google search engines and more freedom on Google+ as well.

User engagement can be gained quiet easily by using this platform for business. Google+ is the only SMM platforms where tens of thousands of influencers are roaming to make sure that they interact with large communities and get benefits of increased fan following and business promotion. A business should try to engage these users on continuous basis as *Google+ is a community that breeds only collaboration and ranks those pages high which are most collaborative with others.* SMM specialist should look for all such collaborators and once they are found hash tags should be used to make sure that they are mentioned in each and every status update. In this way the page will be highlighted in a community which is laser targeted and business can get more and more followers from there without any hassle. This is also a great way to make sure that the business page comes to the eye of these users and they begin collaborating for good of both communities, having thousands of followers mean that there is a sense of mutual as well as business trust and therefore it is very important to get noticed so that members of both communities can make good use of resources of each another to foster their relationships with each another.

- **Private communities** are the best way for a business
  to find those who are aligned with a certain product or
  service. If the business has created a community in this
  manner then new requests from the Google+ followers
  show that they want to be a part of this community in
  order to do something good. The virtual world of
  internet is even faster than the normal life and for the
  same reason no one has time to send requests if he is
  not serious regarding the business or page. It is also
  one of the best ways to laser targeted audience
  however care should be practiced in this regard as a

private community cannot be changed to public or vice versa after it has been created.

- **Engagement** on Google + is one of the best reasons to use this platform for good of business. It means that once a community has been created then the users will automatically get notifications of the status updates that are posted by the page manager on the community wall. It is thus mandatory for all the business page managers to make sure that those posts are shared that have some value or else the users will turn off the notifications or will leave the community which is not the actual target. User engagement through quality content and on time replies and resolutions will make sure that the best is given to the business without much effort.

"No matter you are running a Facebook Fan page, Google+ page or Twitter following the core

mechanics for indulging the customers on social

media platform remain the same."

- **Awesome content management and creation** is also one of the best aspects of using Google+ for business use. Google+ has awesome features like Google hangout and video calling service. A business can get post creation ideas from the private community and can also use Google hangout to make sure that real time ideas are dropped by the followers. Once the process has been completed the thread could be marked archived and the people with the best ideas can be contacted through video calling so that the idea can be generated in the best possible way. These steps make the content creation even unique and better.

- **Complete content control** is one of the best features of Google+. In a business community the content can be preserved by making sure that resharing is disabled and to further secure and control the community the best strategy is to disable the comments so that it becomes view only without any sharing and comments. It is also recommended for a business to create couple of communities as they are free of cost. One of these communities should be gated and other one is to be publicized so that content management and idea capturing is done in a well-defined manner.

- **The Google Analytics** also apply to Google+ and once the business has shared a post it is recommended to get an insight that how many people have shared or reshared a particular post. In this way the public inclination becomes clear and the business is in a position to make sure that great content is created which matches the need as well as demand of the audience. This also makes it possible to spread the word of the business farther as the number of shares will increase if relevant content has been posted keeping in mind the overall mindset of the targeted audience and their demands.

- **Google+ helpdesk** is an idea that has been implemented by large brand and business pages on Google+. Unlike traditional helpdesk the paid employees are not hired to maintain the operations instead those users who are old users of the products or services of the company are hired to get the world to make sure that they remain empower and on the other hand the load on traditional customer services is minimum. It is a rule of thumb that if a user has been empowered in return not only will they work hard but will also make sure that they spread the word of the company in the best possible way. *Expansion of communities on Google+ is never possible till the users are not empowered.*

- **Google+ events** allow the business to celebrate a particular achievement with their customers creates a strong bond of love and affection with the customers. It is a recently launched service of the Google+ and it includes features where a business can send requests for webinars, events, meetings and even hangouts which is a 100 user chat simultaneously. This awesome feature increases the effect of SMM by making sure that the users hosted by the business are again brought to a single platform for explanation or a newly launched product or for celebration of any event. There is a feature of Party mode within this event circle which allows each and every one of the attendants to instantly upload photos of the event through a mobile application and hence a photo journal is created immediately.

- **Posting at least 7 to 10 times a day** is a key to success when it comes to Google+. It is due to the fact that the keywords optimization is indexed in Google search engine as well as it has been explained before. Each and every business post should be such that it makes sure to gather as many users as possible making it easy for the search engine to rank the community and the business on first page of search results. For example the page is related to tires business so once a user enters the keywords like best tires business the page will definitely appear if the right choice of keywords has been made and optimized for building the community. It is also known as *Google social search results*

- **Google authorship** is one of the vital advantages of using Google+ SMM strategy. Google always keeps an eye on the SEO tactics that are being used all around the world so that the website can be ranked high. According to the report published by Forbes in August 2014 almost 90% of total traffic on the internet comes from Google and therefore it is very important to make sure that the posts and the business pages are optimized in such a way so that the aspect of SEO is also preserved. However black hat SEO tactics are never to be used as it will lead to community as well as website blocking by the Google. In order to avoid this hassle it is very important for any business page to get Google Authorship. By acquiring this picture of the author will appear next to the posts and links once they come up in Google search results. Hence a high click through rate as well as element of trust will be built causing the people from outside to join the community. Another benefit that is not known to many SMM specialists is that the page as well as the website is monitored by the Google on continuous basis so there is no issue of blocking. Any illegitimate technique used will be removed by the automated SEO bots of Google even without notifying the user. This is one of the best ways to make sure that page is ranked number 1 according to the terms and conditions that are set by Google.

- **Rich text search** should be used to make sure that all industry related keywords and phrases are searched so that more targeted groups and audience can be searched that drive traffic. It is also advised to save these searches for a future period of time so that they can be repeated time and again in this regard as the results never remain the same. These searches also make sure that those posts mentioning the brand name as well as the industry comes up for better view as well as exposure.

Take a look

43% of the total firms are using social media in a way that is ineffective and are not getting the desired results due to lack of knowledge.

45% of the total corporations are using social media in a way that they some way or the other manage to achieve the targets.

Only 12% of the total business users are using the social media in an optimal manner getting what the target is.

Google+ launches new features

On Google+ it is very important to take part in relevant conversations that are related to the industry. Success never comes to doorstep in this regard and for the same reason it is very important to note that it is the element of interaction with new users outside the community that makes sure that the results driven in a manner that the business requires. A successful business is run only if both personal as well as business accounts are used to attract the users.

Besides Google+ own platform the business should also make sure that the best is taken out of the other services of Google such as YouTube. SMM strategy when it comes to Google+ should be channelized in such a way so that other platforms are also controlled from the Google+ page or community. The subscribers of YouTube channel are also potential clients and most of them are the ones which the business is already hosting. If extra 10 minutes are given each day then business can be flourished to a great extend. It is also important to take forward all the channels in a simultaneous manner. For instance a video should not be uploaded to YouTube till the related conversation on Google+ has not ended. All Google based social media accounts should be integrated so that hassle of multiple posting is never faced.

Using Google+ events webinars should be created to make sure that more questions related to brand or the industry are clarified. Webinar software programs are very expensive and most of small businesses are not able to purchase them so Hangouts On Air are the best alternative in this regard which allows the business page to make sure that live streaming is broadcasted to the YouTube channel in this way this recording can be published separately to the Google+ page making sure that the best is provided to the audience who were absent due to time zone difference. Most of the businesses are unaware of the power of animated videos. In order to launch a new product and service it is recommended to create an animated video with pictures if a business wants its page and the product to go viral. Video minded marketers can get the most of this feature and using the Google+ gated community a business can also make sure that the best ideas are generated from user side in order to get nice and powerful videos. Google+ Auto awesome is the best feature that allows the business to create awesome animated videos in this regard.

LinkedIn

Introduction

Launched in 2003 LinkedIn can be regarded as the most professional social networking platform of the world. Number of daily active users is 300 million so again just like any other social media a large market is there for any business that wants to establish itself using this platform.

General/Optimum use of LinkedIn for SMM

About 20% of total user base of LinkedIn is based on small businesses and for the same reason it is very important for any business to make relations and to make sure that the best is taken out of this platform in form of revenue as well as sales. LinkedIn is definitely a good platform for large corporations but for small businesses it is a boon as most of the features are not just free of charge but they are effective as well as compared to other social media platforms. Following are some ideas that are effective for both large and small corporations:

- **Recommendations** are the best way to ensure that business gain quick reputation over LinkedIn. It can be easily done by providing top notch quality to the customers as well as making sure that indirect marketers are obtained as well. Whenever a customer posts a good review for the business the SMM specialist should request that customer to write a good review as well to make sure that others customers are quickly gained. By using LinkedIn the sole motive of the business should not be to generate revenue but good recommendations should also be included in the core strategy of the business.

- **Business minded users** form at least 70% of total base of LinkedIn. It is therefore very important to take care of these users. LinkedIn is awesome due to the fact that SMM strategy requires minimum status updates in this regard. However it is NEVER recommended to associate LinkedIn with any other social media platform as this is a professional platform for serious business users and therefore it should be kept as it is. The impact of the status updates can however be increased by making optimum use of all LinkedIn features that it offers free of charge.

- **Outsourcing** is a global phenomenon and therefore small businesses can use this platform to transfer services cross border so that they are carried out in a well defined manner. By using LinkedIn premium service a business can also make sure that quotations are demanded from all the vendors that are related to the industry and then the best is chosen among them. However LinkedIn premium is not free and the social media site charges a small amount on monthly basis. This objective of outsourcing can also be achieved by making sure that recommendations from partner businesses are also given priority in this regard. If business already has vendors as connection that personalized messaging service can be used to make sure that individual rates are demanded.

- **Adding business to different groups** is another key to success when it comes to LinkedIn. It is the best way to know latest industry trends as well as associations. These associations breed relationships and as a result potential clients are identified by the business. As of now LinkedIn has a total of 600 groups that are being used by businesses to flourish. There is not a single industry that is not covered by LinkedIn so it is very important for all the businesses to make sure that these groups are joined and visited frequently. It is also to be noted that these groups cover all the industry related events as well so a small business can definitely imagine the effect of visiting such events and finding out potential client base in this regard.

- **Client satisfaction** is never attained till questions are not answered. LinkedIn currently operates almost 2500 groups that are related to small businesses and the questions that customers ask most of the time. So any hard or vexing question can be answered quiet easily by making sure that these groups are tapped in a professional manner.

- **Knowledge sharing** is one of the most awesome ways to gain and attract new clients. It is due to the fact that customers or clients are always inclined towards those businesses that are ready to help and answer their queries. A business can join the groups and can post answers that are related to their area of expertise and when any potential client reads that answer he will surely contact the business so this is another way to make sure that potential clients are dug out of this huge professional network.

- **Crowdfunding** is always needed by small businesses to make sure that a product or service is launched in the best possible way. Crowdfunding is not solely related to cash gain instead it can also be used to name a product, asking customers about design and layout of new guitar and many other ways. A small

business can inject the element of personalization to make sure

that the best is got from all the customers who are following

the business. In monetary terms it can also be a life saver for

the business and according to an estimate there are around

12M small businesses that are ready to provide funding to

other businesses in this regard.

- **Keeping the company page public** is one of the best

solutions to make sure that the customers are getting a deep

insight when into the business and they are also able to delve

deep into the mechanics which the business is following.

Almost 97% companies on LinkedIn have kept their profiles

public and it is also regarded as one of the greatest tools to

capture more clients. It has a dual effect on the business as the

professionals from the industry also contact the business to

offer their services in this regard. The LinkedIn pros also deem

it as one of the best ways to make sure that healthy

competition occupies the industry that also makes business happy.

Specific used of LinkedIn for SMM

- **Quality connections** should be made to make sure that best use of LinkedIn is done in a manner that is also legit. Before sending connection request to any business or potential client the related profile should be examined in such a way so that the legitimacy is crystal clear. A business should beware of all such profiles that are illegitimate or pretend to be a certain business when actually they are not. It will not only save time but if there is any additional cost related to the business it will also make sure that it is also saved in the best interest of the business. A great way to check it out is to make sure that there are at least 150 connections, picture placed o profile is in line with the business requirements and recommendations are there to support the profile as well as the past achievements. It will also make sure that the high number of connections also gets more references in this regard.

- **Immediate message to potential client** is the first and foremost thing that can be done to make sure that potential opportunities are explored going forward. Once a connection has been added then a business should never wait for the message instead it should make sure that the message is sent as soon as possible so that the opportunities are explored without wasting anytime in this regard. If there is a sign of any potential business then it is better to exchange the phone numbers as it will make the connection a more personalized one in this regard.

- **Market examine** is another advantage of using LinkedIn. This social media platform also provides graphs and other valuable insights to make sure that a particular industry is examined in the best possible way. It will make it possible for the business to move forward with a more targeted approach so that best results are obtained over the period of time. The businesses

that were formerly indulged in call calling activities now also

prefer using LinkedIn as this platform allows the business to

contact directly with the clients without any hassle or issue

saving money as well as the manpower expenses. This

platform has undoubtedly changed the demographics of the

business.

- **Advanced search** option is one of the best that makes sure

  that the best clients are targeted when it comes to a specific

  niche. A laser targeted approach in this regard will make sure

  that a business gets the best without any issue or problem. If

  small business is ready to spend some money then premium

  option is most recommended one in this regard. It will allow

  the business to delve deeper into the industry so that more

  potential clients are reached in fewer time.

- **Personalized messages** make sure that the potential customers

  or expected business partners never consider business as a

spam. For every client to whom the business wants to connect the approach should be different. Business should value all those clients that can benefit their business in any way or mean and a BUSINESS MESSAGE should never be sent to them. All messages to such clients should be designed in such a way which makes sure that these clients are not only captured but they also get a feeling that the business values them.

- **All inefficiencies of the business related to social media platform** can be examined by using LinkedIn. There are tens of thousands of groups on LinkedIn where social media experts are offering their services. To make optimal use of LinkedIn profile a business can contact them in this regard to make sure that all profile issues are not only corrected but these issues are also eliminated once and for all. By eradicating these inefficiencies a business can grow the quality client base and can also capture those markets that were hidden due to these inefficiencies.

LinkedIn has been an apple of eye for all those businesses that want to grow their operations using a professional network ad at the same time want to save cost. The acquisitions of LinkedIn are also a way to make sure that clients are captured through various platforms for instance SlideShare which is a renowned content sharing website. It also belongs to LinkedIn and hence it is regarded as the best site to capture clients through a content sharing website. If a business has a content management department as well then it is recommended to manage the content through SlideShare so that the clients can be captured through multiple platforms.

To make sure that the business captures the US market it is again recommended using LinkedIn as according to latest stats that have been published by the network almost 30% of total users i.e. 93 million come from US. This count includes all type of users including the business as well as individuals so to make optimal usage of LinkedIn profile it is recommended to take full advantage of this platform.

The LinkedIn Influencers program was launched in 2012 and through this program total of 300+ professionals are invited to share their ideas in relation to business and its expansion. If the business is newly launched then it is recommended to join and enable the updates of this influencers program as each and every quote of this program can be regarded as gem for all new businesses.

LinkedIn is a de facto tool for all professional marketing and network building as the mechanics that are set by network managers are such that they force all the businesses from around the world to keep the operations on track when it comes to LinkedIn so that the professionalism of the site can be preserved. Using LinkedIn for marketing is a boon as it makes sure to bring businesses and people together so that they can take advantage of each another's expertise in a way that real world environment is felt. Entering the market is never easy but LinkedIn has been the best service provider in this regard.

YouTube

Introduction

Again just like Google+ YouTube is also backed by the power of Google so it is another great platform to make sure that the content is also indexed in Google search engine. It was founded in 2005 i.e. 9 years ago and it serves all the viewers worldwide making its slogan i.e. "Broadcast Yourself" true in every aspect.

Myths about YouTube

- **Virality is a success** and this is the greatest myth in this regard. Reaching more YouTube users never mean that the brand is recognized. Different users and communities are there on YouTube and they would take the business video according to their own perception. Instead of launching a single video it is advised to launch a series of videos instead as first episode will drive potential audience and the number of views on the video will be genuine in terms of pure user base.

- **YouTube creators are very helpful** in some aspects but not all. A business can always be successful on its own when it comes to YouTube. A business should make sure that the channel is optimized in such a way that it conveys the message in full. The collaborations with the YouTube impact groups can be fruitful but to relying on them is never recommended.

- **Utility videos are most impactful** but they are not a key to success. YouTube servers people all over the world so one utility video can and should be launched with different cultural moments. It will make sure that business gets worldwide exposure and on the same time also captures cross border clients.

- **Everyone will watch the business video** but the reality is that most of the channel subscribers don't even know that a video is uploaded. Instead they find new videos from the Google while searching for a business related topic. In this regard the business should keep an eye on the comment feed as they make sure that the video has been appreciated in full even if it has been launched by parts.

YouTube SMM strategies

There are certain algorithms which a business should keep in view to make sure that the YouTube rankings as well as Google search rankings remain at the best for the business. Following are some of the metrics which SMM specialists should use with extreme care so that best results are gained in this regard:

- **Meta data** are technical points which most of the businesses ignore but in HTML programming the Meta tag should be filled with optimized keywords and the description of the tag should not exceed 153 characters in order to rank the YouTube page high.

- **Keyword optimization** should be done for every video so that the best rank is achieved and video is indexed high on Google as well as YouTube search results. The video description should be filled with keywords and as much as possible keywords should be added in this regard. One thing that should be kept in view is that the Meta data keywords should also be placed in description.

- **Location of the business** should also be updated as soon as video is uploaded. Google geo targets certain search results as well so it is the best option for a business to show cast its products to all the people of local area. The channel profile should also have the same location as updated in the videos to get the best results.

- **Annotations** are the best way to ensure that each and every video delivers a call to action. For example a business can request the users to subscribe the channel for more exciting or utility content.

- **Interlinking videos** is also one of the best ways to make sure that the content on the main website is also ranked high. The other links to the videos are often converted to hyperlinks and they make sure that the main business website ranking also improves and gets even better in Google index.

- **YouTube insights** should be monitored and measured on continuous basis to track the changes. If it is done not only the video quality improves but the business will also learn various other techniques that are required to rank the video high on both YouTube and Google. Google analytics can also be used as a part to make sure that the best is provided to business YouTube channel in terms of Google rankings.

- **Playlists should be created** once the business has planned to release a series of videos. It will definitely make sure that the users are indulged as these playlists also come up in YouTube as well as Google search results. The element of curiosity will also be injected and the users will wait for the next episode eagerly and top fans will definitely give good comments

making the video active.

- **Thumbnails** are limited by YouTube but still to make sure

  that a good view of the video is provided to the viewers it is

  recommended to get a good thumbnail for the video that shows

  the most attractive part so that more clicks, comments and

  views make the video noisy and business should also consider

  the fact that noisy videos are always ranked very high on

  YouTube.

YouTube has transformed the world of business and the organizations

which were faceless once can now show their faces to the world in a

manner that makes it possible for them to gain more customers and insights

on their products. As it is a known fact that social media users are really

smart people and therefore they all are looking forward to get good brands on board so that they can collaborate with their videos to make sure that they get the best products while sitting at home. Business should use the channel as a landing page so that the subscribers are captured in a manner that makes them loyal and also makes sure that they remain intact with the channel in form of permanent subscribers bringing in more customers.

Business mechanics and SMM

In the wake of advancement in science and technology it is inevitable for every business to make sure that SMM is regarded as the core marketing strategy in this regard. The best and the most effective business is the one that has a strong social media management team and on the other hand it also has a strong grip on the social media and the users it has. According to analysis done in this regard it is very important to note that almost *half of the population of the world is connected with social media.* Hence the business cannot flourish if this awesome platform is not captured. Using simple tips and strategies can lead awesome results in this regard and it is also to be noted that a good SMM team is one that has developed strategies which affect the business for long term. According to Facebook insights they are keen to get almost 3 billion users till the end of 2015 so if this medium is captured then success is not a big deal at all. Above all it is very important to know that SMM strategy cannot be implemented alone. It is can and should be implemented in line with the online marketing strategy so that the best is taken out of SMM strategy that is implemented. For all new businesses it is very important to know what mechanics are being implemented or developed by the large companies who are highly successful on social media. It is also a reality that most of the large companies do not have to do much when it comes to SMM because they have an established name in the market which also allows them to get ahead of others in a smart manner and without much effort. On the other hand a small business has to do a lot in order to make sure that they establish their reputation on social media so the first thing which they need to provide is customer satisfaction and secondly in order to succeed on social media it is very important to make sure that the related business page always remain noisy and full of life. Continuous activities on the page mean that the users are very active and on the other hand they are brand loyal. SMM strategy for any business should not solely base on the social media team. Top users from the page should be selected to make sure that exclusive rights are given to them so that they can manage the page. Each and every such user should be chosen with respect to time difference so that the page is also managed 24/7. It is also very important for any business to make sure that it is getting the best results when it comes to brand establishment. It has been seen that only those businesses that have established themselves as a brand are most successful on social media. Clear focus as well as timely implementation of all strategies makes sure that a business remains successful on the social media forever. A business should be well versed about all the relevant issues that it can face on social media so experienced team should be hired in this regard. An important thing to remember is that if the business team does not have enough capabilities then it is recommended to outsource the social media management as it is not a place for experiments so everything should be planned and executed in a well-defined manner to make sure that the best is given to the business in the long run.

For a business the social media is not a place for being social rather it is more of a network. The two concepts are entirely different so they should not be interrelated in any regard. Business should be clear in this regard that being social is always second to networking and hence it is very important to know the difference and it is the only point that would make the overall SMM strategy successful as well as dominating for the competitors.

Social media strategy is not an easy thing to develop and maintain over a longer period of time so it is really important to know that the real and very hard work is needed in this regard as once built reputation on social media can be hampered if an even small mistake is committed so a business should always keep the things to the point so that the success is enjoyed in the long run otherwise there are *many competitors in the market who are ready to take the top position and are just waiting for a chance in this regard.*

Large business corporations make sure that always two pages are created on social media where one is used to develop the strategies, generating ideas through crowdfunding and the main page is used for execution of all such strategies. Making a business page in this way makes sure that success is never farfetched. Some common mistakes in SMM are as follows:

- Waiting too much to launch a product or a service.

- Solving issues that are not important at all.

- Customers are not given importance as they demand.

- Not answering the questions of the common page user.

- Actively starting a discussion and then becoming stagnant.

The points above are very important and can be regarded as crux of SMM strategy. If implemented in a good manner then they can lead to awesome results and if ignored then there is no one responsible for the failure but the business itself. Adhering to the points will also make sure that the social media pace is never thwarted by these issues as they will be taken care of if an active approach is adopted. Each and every move on the social media should be laser targeted to make sure that the nothing is off the track. SMM gurus are also of the view that one off track move on social media can be dangerous so a professional business profile on any platform should

avoid this at any cost.